Carme Solé Vendrell
Josep Mª Parramón

summer

Parramón

Summer is the time when the sun smiles

The meadows are full of lovely coloured flowers

The fruit ripens on the trees

No one wants to stay indoors so the shops are often closed

It's the time for going on holiday

The fields are gold with corn

There are beautiful sunsets

Children play on the beach, making sandcastles and swimming

Or you can take a boat out to sea

**The hot weather
makes everyone thirsty**

...and they lie in the sunshine
and relax

It's summer!

SUMMER

The summer solstice
On the twenty-first of June every year the sun is at its highest point in the sky. This means that the night is the shortest of the year and the day the longest. In ancient times people celebrated this day at Stonehenge.

The sun grows warmer, fruit ripens
In July, August and September as the days grow warmer, all the delicious soft fruits ripen and become ready to eat. Strawberries and raspberries, cherries peaches and plums, followed by blackberries and pears.

Schools close — it's holiday time
Every school child has a lovely long holiday in the summer. No getting up early, no homework, no lessons, no teachers — just having fun at home instead.

Shops close, people travel
Lots of small businesses close for a week or two in the summer so that the people who work in them can take some time off. They take to the roads in their cars or fly abroad to see new places and meet new people.

The farmer's work is never done
In the country, however, it is a time of work. The harvest has to be gathered and the farmer has to labour hard in the long, hot days. Wheat is one of the main crops — from it we make bread, cereal, flour and cakes.

Summer is the hottest season of the year
It gets lovely and hot in the summer and people wear light clothes. Women wear pretty sleeveless dresses and men take off their jackets and roll up their shirt-sleeves. Those who live near the sea go swimming, others like to go the seaside for their holidays. Favourite food in hot weather? Ice-cream!

Summer is a happy time
In summer, because of the good weather and the long light evenings, people spend more time out of doors enjoying themselves. Some play summer sports such as cricket while others enjoy swimming, walking or gardening. Summer is a time of good health and happiness. Three cheers for the sun! Three cheers for summer!